Bug Life

Funny & Weird

Insect Animals

Funny & Weird Animals Series

By

P. T. Hersom

This book is dedicated to my grandson Cameron who has always been afraid of most bugs. I think once he sees how funny and weird bugs can be, he will lose his fear of them.

Love ya, Cameron!

Bug Life Funny & Weird Insect Animals by P. T. Hersom

© Copyright 2013 P. T. Hersom, All rights reserved

No part of this publication may be reproduced, distributed or transmitted in any form or by any means, including photocopying, recording or other electronic or mechanical methods, without the prior written permission of this publisher, except in the case of brief quotations embodied in critical reviews and certain other noncommercial uses permitted by copyright law. For permission requests, write to the publisher.

Hersom House Publishing, 3365 NE 45th St, Suite 101

Ocala, Florida 34479 USA

What are Bugs?	5
Altas Moth	8
Banana Spider	10
Bombardier Beetle	12
Camel Spider	14
Dragonfly	16
Gallinipper	18
Giant Isopod	20
Giant Water Bug	22
Giant Weta	24
Goliath Beetle	26
Japanese Giant Hornet	28
Katydid or Bush Cricket	30
Lantern Fly	32
Leaf Insect	34
Leaf Insect	34
Lightning Bug or Firefly	36
Monarch Butterfly	38
Panda Ant	40

Peanut Head Lantern Fly..42

Peruvian Giant Yellow-leg Centipede 44

Praying Mantis 46

Scorpionfly 48

Stink Bug 50

Thorn Bug...52

Walking Stick..54

What Did You Learn Today? Questions 56

What Did You Learn Today? Answers 58

Other Books to Enjoy by P. T. Hersom 60

Enjoyed the Book? 63

What are Bugs?

Bugs can be funny looking and do some very weird things, but what are bugs? Well some bugs for example are butterflies, spiders, beetles, ants, and bees; some bugs fly, while others creepy crawl, and all bugs scoot around on six or eight, or even more legs.

All insects are bugs, but not all bugs are insects. Insects have three body parts, the head, the middle called the thorax, and the abdomen. They also have two antennas on their head and three pair of legs, for a total of six legs.

Spiders are not insects; they have eight legs and no antennas. Neither are scorpions or centipedes, they have eight or more legs, but they are bugs.

Most bugs start life by hatching from an egg, most insects as larvae or nymphs. Larvae are insect worms, for example caterpillars and maggots are larvae. While nymphs, unlike most larvae, live in the same environment and eat the same food as adults. Many insect nymphs live in the water and have special structures like gills or swimming legs.

Further growth is controlled by their skeleton, which is on the outside of their body and called an exoskeleton. With their skeletons on the outside, and their soft parts inside, growing up is difficult.

Every time they want to grow, they have to break out of their exoskeleton and swell up to a larger size before their new skin hardens. This process is called molting and means once the insect is an adult it can't grow any bigger.

Moth and butterfly caterpillars go through metamorphosis, in this time period the caterpillars form a cocoon around themselves made of silk and then their inside parts change drastically. When they break out of the cocoon they have now changed into a moth or butterfly.

The scientists that study insects and help us understand what bugs are all about, are called entomologists.

Altas Moth

Where they live: Tropical forest of Southeast Asia.

What they like to eat: Leaves and foliage of evergreen and citrus trees.

Tell Me More

The Atlas Moth is known to be the largest moth in the world due to its huge wings; wingspans up to 10 in/25 cm are commonly recorded. It was named after the titan, Atlas of Greek mythology. In Asia were the moth lives, it's also known by another name which in Cantonese means snake's head moth. If you look at the moth's wing tips you can see how they look like snake heads. This is a natural defensive system to ward off predators, for when the moth flaps its wings, the tips appear to be snakes moving back and forth.

Adult moths never get to eat. They solely live off the baby fat they stored up while eating as a caterpillar. As a moth, their mouth never fully forms all its parts, so they only live about two weeks. Now that's weird!

Banana Spider

Where they live: Coastland and swampy regions all over the world.

What they like to eat: Mainly insects, but have been known to eat small birds and snakes.

Tell Me More

Known for their zigzag patterned large webs, the Banana Spider is also known as the Golden Silk Orb-Weaver, this is because the silk in which the spiders make their webs, shines like gold in the sunlight. These golden cobwebs have been harvested to make silk garments such as the golden cape shown.

They do produce venom similar to the black widow spider, to incapacitate their prey, but it's not as potent or harmful to humans.

Bombardier Beetle

Where they live: In the grass and woods all over the world.

What they like to eat: Insects.

Tell Me More

Bombardier's get their name from their ability to shoot hot lethal spray out of their butt. This is the way they protect themselves against enemies. I guess you could say, it's kind of like a "bug fart" because it makes a popping sound when they do it!

This bug fart happens when two chemicals, hydrogen peroxide and hydroquinone, come together with catalytic enzymes and water which are all store separately inside the bug's gut until needed. When the bug feels threatened the chemicals all mix together and create a hot toxic gas, which shoots out hitting any attackers.

This bug fart can kill other bugs, and if some were to get on your skin it could sting a little. Some bombardiers have the ability to bug fart in many directions at the same time. I bet that took some practice.

Camel Spider

Where they live: Dry desert climates of the world.

What they like to eat: Bugs and small animals.

Tell Me More

Recognized by their scary and weird appearance the Camel Spider can grow up to 8 in/20 cm across. It's a very fast mover with speeds up to 10 mph/16 km/h, that's fast for a bug!

Camel Spiders get their name from hanging out in places where camels do, in dry desert areas. They are not poisonous, but their bite can be very painful.

Dragonfly

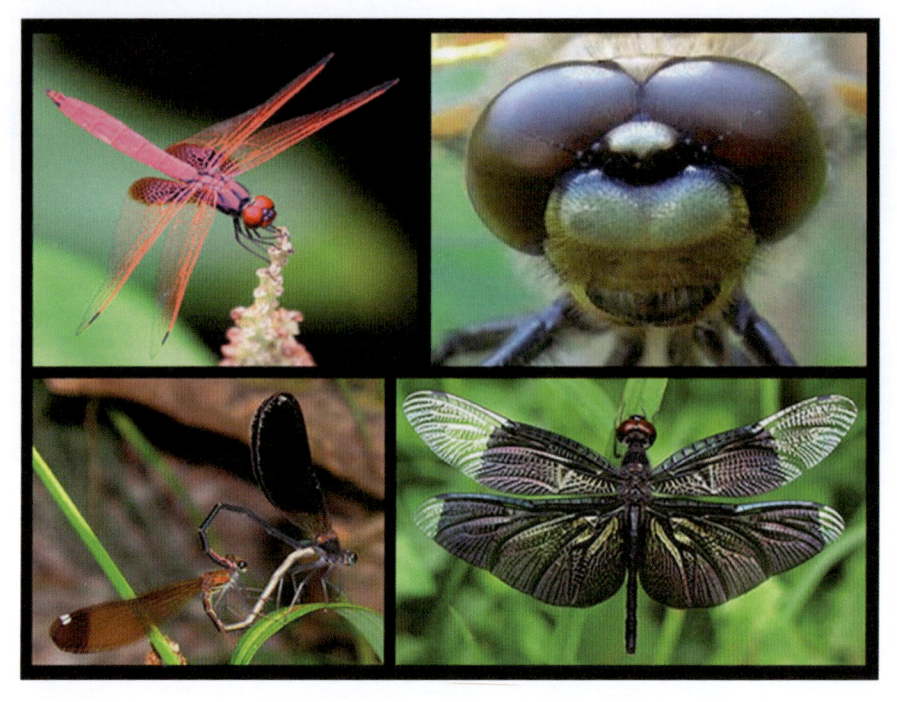

Where they live: Around water and wetlands all over the world.

What they like to eat: Insects.

Tell Me More

Dragonflies are predators, which mean they like to eat other insects. They play an important role for us humans because they especially like to eat mosquitoes and flies.

They can fly just like a helicopter from side to side, up, down, forward and backwards. Plus is one of the fastest flying bugs in the world with speeds up to 60 mph/ 97 km/h, and although have six legs, they can't walk very well.

Dragonflies lay their eggs in or near water. When they hatch, the larvae or babies are called "nymphs" and live in the water. Dragonflies actually live most of their lives in the water as nymphs, feeding on mosquitoes, fish and tadpoles. The funny thing is they have gills on their butt, which they use to breathe with just like a fish. And when they want to go really fast underwater they shoot water out their butt!

When it's time for the nymph to change into a dragonfly, it crawls out of the water. The skin begins to split open behind its head. This is called molting. Then the dragonfly crawls out of the old skin and shakes its wings to dry them off, and then flies away as a new dragonfly.

Gallinipper

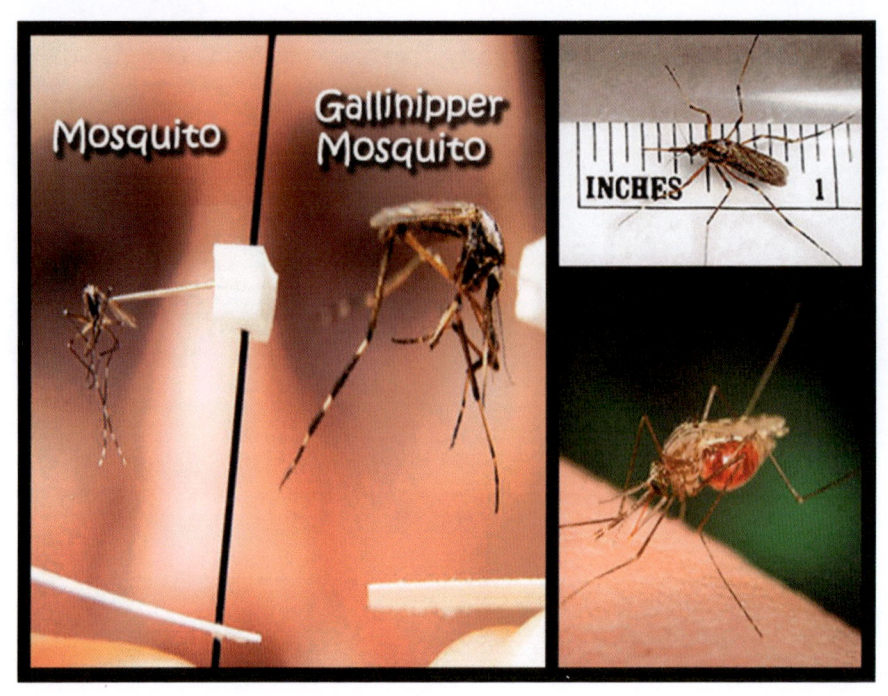

Where they live: East of the Continental Divide in North America.

What they like to eat: Blood from animals and people.

Tell Me More

Gallinippers are large mosquitoes, ready to take a bite of you! These mosquitoes are not only big, but very aggressive too, towards humans and animals. They must dilute the blood of their prey, with their spit before they can drink it. The Gallinipper's spit is what makes the bite itch.

Never fear though, the same bug spray keeps these mosquitoes away just like the others. Plus their bite doesn't sting as much and they do not spread the dreaded West Nile virus as other mosquitoes.

Giant Isopod

Where they live: In the deep cold regions of the Atlantic, Indian and Pacific Oceans.

What they like to eat: Dead fish, whales and squid.

Tell Me More

Giant Isopods are bugs that live in the ocean and are related to crabs and shrimp, however, they are also related to the land dwelling insect pill bug and the common woodlouse. Much like the woodlouse, they have their skeleton on the outside of their body, called an exoskeleton. Which has overlapping segments and when they curl up; they look just like a ball.

They are scavengers which mean they like to eat leftovers and dead things. You might think of them as "trash men of the sea" because they go around eating up the things other fish don't want to eat, thus keeping the ocean clean.

Giant Water Bug

Where they live: In freshwater streams and ponds all around the world.

What they like to eat: Fish, crayfish, frogs, snakes and small turtles.

Tell Me More

These giant bugs are also called by the names Toe-biter and Alligator Fleas. Known for being good hunters, these bugs like to hang out on the bottom of the pond or stream lying motionless until food swims by, then ka-powie! They make a strike on their prey with their piercing mouth, injecting a digestive spit into the victim. This turns the bitten area into a liquefied mush.

The Giant Water Bug's bite is considered to be the most painful insect bite in the world! So don't get one for a pet.

The eggs of the Giant Water Bug are laid on the male bug's wings and then he carries them around until they hatch. When approached by a potential threat they "play dead" and "poop their pants" by releasing a fluid from their butt, and stay still until the danger has passed.

Giant Weta

Where they live: In New Zealand.

What they like to eat: Plants and insects.

Tell Me More

The Giant Weta is found only in the country of New Zealand and mainly on its outlining islands. It's not only very big for an insect, but is the heaviest of all insects on earth, one bug weighing 2.5 ounces/72 grams. They are nocturnal, which mean they like to play at night and their wingspans average around 7 in/18 cm.

They are friendly and harmless to humans.

Goliath Beetle

Where they live: Tropical forest of Africa.

What they like to eat: Fruit and tree sap.

Tell Me More

Named after Goliath from the bible, these beetles are some of the largest insects in the larvae stage, weighing as much as 3.5 oz/100 gm and up to 10in/250 cm in length.

Goliath beetles, like almost all other beetles, have a rock-hard first pair of wings called elytra, they act as a protective shield for their secondary pair of wings. Only the second pair of wings is actually used for flying.

Japanese Giant Hornet

Where they live: Japan.

What they like to eat: Insects.

Tell Me More

These guys are mean and big, growing up to 1.6 in/4 cm in length and having a wingspan of 2.5 in/6 cm. Its Japanese name actually means "giant sparrow bee". They live in hives like bees do and have workers that go out to kill insects, to bring back as food for the hive. Then chew up the killed insects into a paste and feed it to the larvae.

The larvae then produce a fluid that is kind of like a supercharged energy drink that the workers eat. This fluid energizes the workers so that they can fly up to 25 mph/40 km/h and distances of 62 miles/100 km in a day! Scientists have learned to make this type of fluid and it is now used in dietary supplements.

The Japanese Giant Hornet likes to kill honey bees and eat their honey. One hornet can kill 40 European honey bees in one minute, so if several hornets were able to get into a bee hive they could easily wipe out the entire hive within hours.

However, the Japanese honey bee has learned how to defend themselves against the hornet attacks. When a hornet comes around the bee hive, the bees come out of their hive in an angry swam, usually containing about 500 bees. They all hop on the hornet forming a ball around it; the bees beat their wings which forces air over their bodies, pushing warm air inside the bee ball. The temperature of the ball rises to 117 °F/47 C. The hornet cannot survive temperatures that hot, but the bees can, so the hornet is killed and the bees save their hive.

Stay away from these guys, their sting is very painful and requires medical treatment. On average 40 people a year die from being stung, largely due to the huge amount of venom they can inject into a person.

Katydid or Bush Cricket

Where they live: Mainly in tropical regions all over the world.

What they like to eat: Seeds, flowers, leaves, bark, snails and insects.

Tell Me More

Katydids have camouflage and mimic colors and shapes that are similar to leaves. Male Katydids have an organ located on their front wings that allow them to produce a sound similar to a cricket.

Lantern Fly

Where they live: Tropical regions all over the world.

What they like to eat: Plant sap.

Tell Me More

How do you catch a lantern bug? Wait for him to run out of gas.

These guys have what appears to be one big nose. However, what looks like a nose is really an extended mouth so that these plant feeding bugs can suck the sap from plants.

The bug's amazing and brilliant appearance didn't go ignored, even folklore attributes magical powers to the bug. It was often believed that lantern bugs are able to create light, like glow worms or fireflies. But their wing patterns merely reflect light, appearing as if they're glowing at night.

Leaf Insect

Where they live: In South Asia and Australia.

What they like to eat: Fruit and plants.

Tell Me More

Leaf Insects are also known by the name "Walking Leaves", you can probably see why. Their natural ability to mimic a leaf is truly astonishing. Using this camouflage to take on the appearance of a leaf, they are able to hide from predators. So precisely that predators often aren't able to tell them apart from real leaves. With some Leaf Insects the edge of the bug's body even has the look of bite marks. In addition, when it walks, it rocks back and forth, to appear like a real leaf blowing in the wind.

Lightning Bug or Firefly

Where they live: Worldwide around wet woodlands, marshes and tropical areas.

What they like to eat: Insects, plant nectar and pollen.

Tell Me More

Lightning Bugs are winged beetles that are also called Fireflies because of their glowing butt that produces a "cold light" to attract mates or prey. Cold light means that there are no ultraviolet or infrared frequencies, this is chemically produced inside their body and not hot to the touch.

Their light flashes on and off, and in patterns that are distinctive to each species. Each blinking pattern is a signal that helps Lightning Bugs find mates. Entomologists are not sure how the bugs control the blinking of their lights on and off.

Monarch Butterfly

Where they live: North America, Australia, New Zealand and Western Europe.

What they like to eat: Plant nectar.

Tell Me More

Monarchs are known for their yearly migration over long distances, just like many birds that fly south to warmer climates in the winter. In North America, beginning in August they gather into enormous southward migrations, and then in the spring they fly back north. The monarch is the only butterfly that flies both north and south every year in North America.

However, no single butterfly makes the whole round trip. Females lay eggs during the migration for the next generation to continue the trip, usually taking 3 to 4 life spans of butterflies.

Panda Ant

Where they live: In dry desert like climates worldwide.

What they like to eat: Plant nectar.

Tell Me More

The Panda ant is not actually an ant, but a wingless wasp! Their real name is Velvet Ant, named after the hairy females that come in many colors like gold, silver, black and white. The black and white colored ones look very similar to a giant panda bear, and that's why they're called Panda Ants.

The males have wings to fly with and are larger than the females, but both make chirping sounds when frightened and have a very painful sting. So don't pick one up!

Peanut Head Lantern Fly

Where they live: In Central and South America.

What they like to eat: Tree sap and resin.

Tell Me More

Also known as the Alligator Bug and Snake Cicada, these peanut headed insects can be up to 3 in/8 cm long, with long snouts on their heads that look similar to a lizard or snake. This can appear very scary, but actually the peanut head insect is a harmless plant hopper that has a straw for a mouth and doesn't even bite.

When threatened, it protects itself by spreading its wings which have fake eyes on them, and then releases chemicals that have a "skunk-like smell" produced from the resins it eats.

Peruvian Giant Yellow-leg Centipede

Where they live: In the tropical rainforest of South America and the Caribbean.

What they like to eat: Snakes, mice, birds, frogs, lizards and insects.

Tell Me More

This giant centipede is known to be very aggressive and feeds on almost anything it encounters, if it can kill it. Using sharp claws it penetrates its prey with toxic venom which is deadly to insects and most small animals. However not usually fatal to people, it can be very painful, and cause chills and fever.

This 46 legged monster can grow up to 18 in/46 cm long, making it the largest centipede in the world. It's a fast mover and with all these legs can climb just about anything and even hang upside down. In recent years they have become popular as exotic pets. No thank you, I'll stick with my dog Scooby Doo!

Praying Mantis

Where they live: In temperate tropical climates worldwide.

What they like to eat: Insects.

Tell Me More

The Praying Mantis gets its name from folding its front legs in the shape of someone praying, as shown in the picture on the right. In the picture on the left we have a Praying Mantis showing the threat display. During this the bug rears back, then spreads its wings and front legs, and holds its mouth wide open. Looks more funny than scary, but I guess it scares away bugs.

They are ambush hunters, and stand still until prey walks near; camouflaged to look much like the plants and twigs they are hiding among.

Scorpionfly

Where they live: Near wetlands of North America.

What they like to eat: Dead insects, pollen, fruit and nectar.

Tell Me More

This bug is known for its scorpion-like looking stinger at the end of its tail. However it is not a stinger, having two claspers on it, the male uses its tail for holding the female while mating.

Courtship is one of giving gifts. The male first attracts a female by releasing a pheromone scent which brings her near, and then offers her a bug dinner he has earlier caught. If she accepts the bug, they'll go on a date. But if she doesn't, he must find a bigger bug to bring to her. Very weird.

Stink Bug

Where they live: Asia and North America.

What they like to eat: Fruits, vegetables and plants.

Tell Me More

Farmers don't like Stink Bugs very much, that's because they like to eat fruit and vegetable crops that the farmers grow. These agricultural pest are not native to North America, but hitched a ride on ships coming from the Far East so it has few natural predators there.

Getting its name from the ability to release a stinky odor that smells like cilantro, the bug uses this as a defense against being eaten by lizards and birds. If you tried to pick one up or move it around, you'll probably get a big whiff of this stinky stuff!

Thorn Bug

Where they live: Florida, Mexico, Central and South America.

What they like to eat: Sap of fruit and ornamental trees.

Tell Me More

These colorful little bugs love to chew on trees, especially fruit trees. So look out fruit growers. Thorn bugs can so heavily cover a tree that it may be difficult to place a finger anywhere on the trunk without touching one. They like to suck the sap and this can cause a lot of damage to the tree.

If you like to go barefooted don't run around these guys, because their spines can easily poke through into your foot. Ouch! That wouldn't be funny, but they do look weird.

Walking Stick

Where they live: In warmer climates all over the world.

What they like to eat: Plants.

Tell Me More

Having one of the most effective natural camouflages in the world, the Walking Stick insect mimic their surroundings appearing as a stick, colored in brown or green.

Many Walking Sticks will play dead to fool an enemy, and some will lose the occasional leg to escape an enemy's grip, while others can release a rotten smelling fluid.

What Did You Learn Today? Questions

1. The Atlas Moth is the smallest moth in the world, true or false?
2. Do Banana Spiders like to eat bananas?
3. "Fire in the Hole" could refer to this beetle, what is its name?
4. Camel Spiders like to ride on camels, true or false?
5. Is there an insect nymph that has gills on its butt?
6. Do Gallinippers like to suck your blood?
7. These bugs can curl up into a ball and their name sounds like iPod, who are they?
8. The Giant Water Bug when scared will play dead and poop its pants, true or false?
9. The Giant Weta looks like a big grasshopper and only lives in what country on earth?
10. The Goliath Beetle has the largest larvae, growing up to 10 in/250 cm long, true or false?
11. I speak Japanese and love to chew up honey bees, what is my name?
12. I look like a leaf and can sound like a cricket, what is my name?
13. The Lantern Fly can light up at night just like the Firefly, true or false?

14. Leaf Insects can actually look like a walking leaf, true or false?
15. I'm a Firefly and I can make my butt light up, what is my other name?
16. I'm the only butterfly in North America that flies south for the winter, what is my name?
17. The Panda Ant is really a baby bear, true or false?
18. The Peanut Head Lantern Fly likes to eat boiled peanuts, true or false?
19. I'm a centipede with 46 legs and 18 in/46 cm long, what is my name?
20. What insect goes to church?
21. Is the Scorpionfly poisonous?
22. What does the Stink Bug's odor smell like?
23. I like to suck tree sap and I'm thorny, what is my name?
24. You can't see a twig run, but you can see a walking stick, true or false?

What Did You Learn Today? Answers

1) True.
2) No, they mainly eat insects.
3) The Bombardier Beetle.
4) False, they live in desert places like camels do.
5) Yes, the Dragonfly nymph!
6) Yes, they are huge mosquitoes and suck blood like a vampire.
7) The Giant Isopod.
8) True.
9) New Zealand.
10) True.
11) The Japanese Giant Hornet.
12) The Katydid or Bush Cricket.
13) False, they do not light up at all.
14) True, they are also known by the name Walking Leaves.
15) The Lightning Bug.
16) The Monarch Butterfly.
17) False, the Panda Ant is really a wasp and the males have wings.
18) False, but it does like to eat tree sap and resin.
19) The Peruvian Giant Yellow-leg Centipede, the largest in the world.
20) The Praying Mantis.

21) No, even though it has a tail that appears to be a scorpion stinger, it's not.

22) The herb cilantro.

23) The Thorn Bug.

24) True, you can see the Walking Stick insect.

Other Books to Enjoy by P. T. Hersom

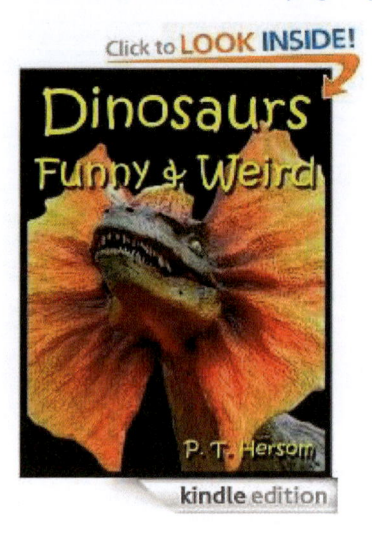

Dinosaurs Funny & Weird Extinct Animals

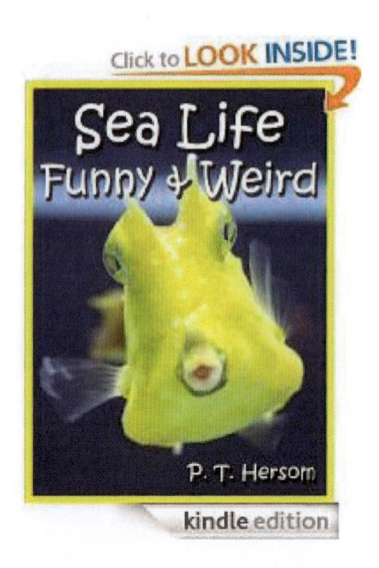

Sea Life Funny & Weird Marine Animals

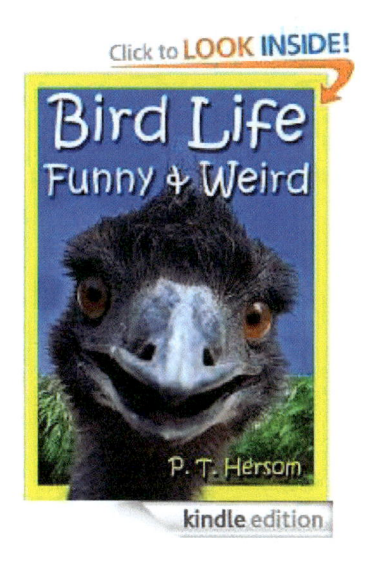

Bird Life Funny & Weird Feathered Animals

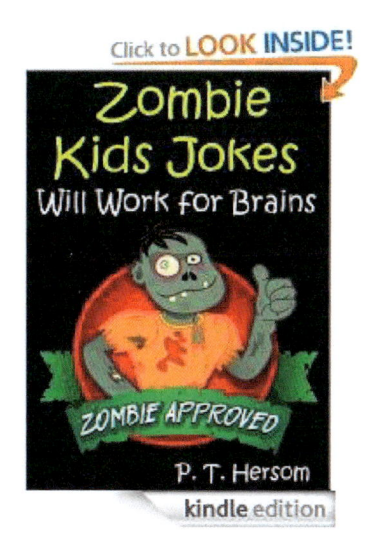

Zombie Jokes: Will Work for Brains

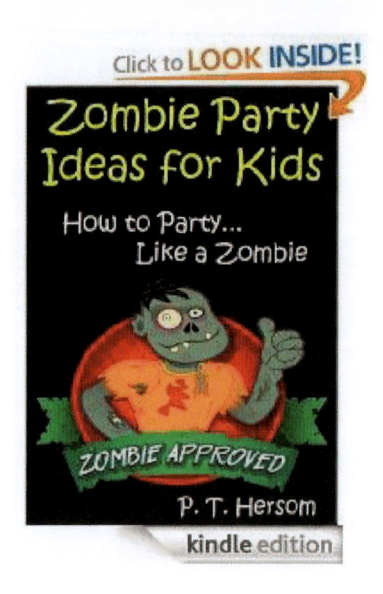

Zombie Party Ideas for Kids: How to Party Like a Zombie

Enjoyed the Book?

Thank you for buying this book. I hope that you and your children enjoy reading the book and learning about the animals in the book as much as I did writing it. If you found the book enjoyable, please help me out by posting a review on the Amazon page. Thank you for taking the time to do so. It is very much appreciated.

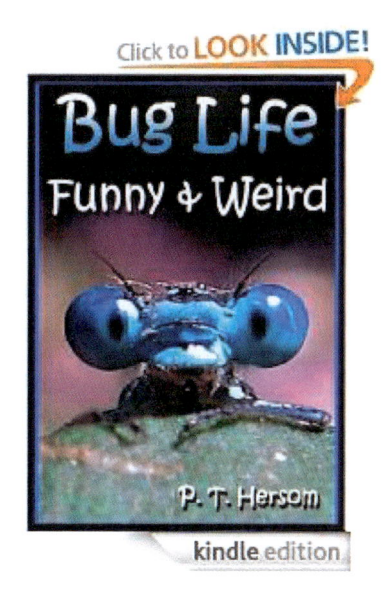

Printed in Great Britain
by Amazon